CENTRAL UNION
OF EUROPE

CENTRAL UNION

of

EUROPE

by [George Harrison]
and *By* PETER JORDAN

INTRODUCTION

By ERNEST MINOR PATTERSON, Ph.D.

*President, The American Academy of Political
and Social Science*

NEW YORK

ROBERT M. McBRIDE & COMPANY

AMERICAN BOOK-STRATFORD PRESS, INC., NEW YORK

INTRODUCTION

By ERNEST MINOR PATTERSON, Ph.D.

*President, The American Academy of Political
and Social Science*

READERS of this eloquent plea for "Central Union" will
have in mind the various possibilities that may be considered. (1) At the one extreme, there is the idea of self-
determination with fifty or sixty or perhaps more countries
all retaining as much sovereignty and independence as is
possible in an interdependent world. (2) At the other extreme is a world federation ultimately to include all countries, each surrendering a considerable part of its sovereignty. (3) There is the proposal that regional groupings
be arranged either with or without each of the groups being dominated by a world organization.

In *Central Union of Europe*, Mr. Jordan advocates the
third of these proposals. In doing so, he is in line with
the most constructive thinking of the day. He is also a
realist in not advocating too strong a federation of the
world or even a federation of Europe. No matter what may
be true in the distant future, the time has not come when

5

great nations will formally surrender any large part of their sovereignty to a world government. Nor is it possible to organize a Federation of Europe until there is no longer fear of its dominance by Germany.

An intermediate step is found in the union of existing countries whose geographical location is suitable and which have an aggregate of population and of resources that furnish an adequate combination for strength. Many such groupings have been suggested with many tests applied. To any one of them objections may be advanced. In every case, difficulties abound, but between the certain disasters of the old world disorder and our unpreparedness for a strong world order, the regional organization is the one that seems to be most nearly feasible and at the same time a step forward. If such groupings can be formed, there is still left the question of their relations to each other, if we are not merely to have new and perhaps more terrible rivalries between the various large regions.

Much depends upon the nature of the groupings that may be arranged. The combination suggested by Mr. Jordan has much to commend it. Its present population seems adequate; its area is sufficient; it abounds in natural resources of great variety; and there is a distinct though not extreme diversity in economic development. With the world so interdependent as it is in the twentieth century, Central Union would not and could not be entirely self-sufficient; but complete self-sufficiency is neither feasible nor desirable.

"The establishment of the Central Union will not be an easy task. The obstacles are numerous and some of them appear at the time of writing to be almost unsurmountable, but this should not be a deterrent." This admission by the author is recorded near the end of the volume and is to be commended. The task is difficult and each day seems to make some of the obstacles more formidable. In a continent so affected by war as is the Europe of today military and political changes are coming almost literally by the hour. In the face of these changes, rigid plans can not be prepared long in advance. The advance of the armies of Russia and the collapse of Germany may result in commitments that will irrevocably alter the position of (say) Eastern Poland and of East Prussia for many years to come. The future of Bessarabia and of Northern Bukovina can not now readily be forecast, but there will apparently still be a Poland and a Roumania and a Czechoslovakia, perhaps with some modifications of borders. No one can at present predict with confidence the future of some of the others, notably that of the Baltic states.

There are at present two groups of countries to be considered. Like the Big Four at the discussions in Paris twenty-five years ago, there are four great Powers today. Not the same group, for France and Italy are missing while in their places are the Soviet Union and China. But now the voices of the smaller nations are being heard. In the interval between the two world wars, their restlessness grew. Though overshadowed by the larger countries their

7

protests increased and from time to time definitely affected the decisions made. Yet, both within the League of Nations and outside, the impotence of the weak states was evident. Witness the tragedy of Abyssinia in the clash with Italy, the failure to aid China when Manchuria was seized by Japan, the sacrifice of Czechoslovakia in the futile effort to appease Germany and the betrayal of Loyalist Spain. No longer are the governments of the great states disposed to ignore them so fully as in the past. Spokesmen for Belgium, Norway, the Netherlands and the Latin American countries have enough in common, because of their size if for no other reason, to make themselves heard and in many matters they are heeded. At the Food Conference in Hot Springs, at Atlantic City when the United Nations Relief and Rehabilitation Administration was organized, and in the discussions about a Currency Union and a Bank for Reconstruction and Development their influence has been felt.

For this there are excellent reasons. As Mr. Jordan points out, few if any small countries can maintain a really independent existence! He says, "The era of small countries seems to be over!" This is, however, true in varying degrees of all countries; even large nations are no longer able to ignore their growing dependence on each other. Though the interests of smaller countries frequently clash, they are increasingly conscious of common interests even while they recognize that their future is strongly dependent on the sufferance of the Great Powers. On the other hand, the larger nations need the smaller ones, if only as a curb upon each other. In addition, there is enough idealism even in international politics to prevent an entirely ruthless attitude to the small and the weak.

Thoughtful readers will not underestimate either present or future difficulties. First, it will be realized that economics and politics are too closely intermingled for either to be discussed without reference to the other. Economic dependence is not merely a matter of nearness as the people of the United States have realized during the past few years. For the sake of its automobile and other industries, the union to which the United States might belong would include the East Indies. Its dependence on tin suggests Malaya and Bolivia, while manganese calls for a union with Brazil and the Soviet Union. No matter what combinations of countries may be brought together because of their proximity to each other, economic dependence will continue. Nothing short of a world union can eliminate it.

Then there is the matter of the balance of power. Before 1914, there was something that went by that name between the Triple Alliance—Germany, Austria, Hungary and Italy; and the Triple Entente—Great Britain, France and Russia. One may properly wonder whether peace would be any better preserved by having five or six combinations or "unions" with interests that are in perpetual conflict.

If such a group of unions is to be a preliminary for a European federation, with or without Great Britain or the Soviet Union, there is still the perplexing question of the relations between a federation of Europe and the rest of the world. The writers on geo-politics—Mackinder, Haushofer and Spykman—have given us "ample food for thought." What, for example, would be the position of the United States if such a union were formed? Even if all the American states were loyal members of an American union, rivalries with other parts of the world would continue and clashes would be probable. Again, there seems to be no ultimate safety short of an organization that would include the entire world.

But Mr. Jordan realizes we must start from where we are. In the United States our political leaders, who presumably are aware of the state of public opinion, are careful to avoid any proposals for the sacrifice of sovereignty to a world government. In the field of close political organization, we are driven back to the Jordan thesis. While the area he has chosen for his proposed union bristles with formidable difficulties, the same can be said of other unions to a greater or a less degree. Union will not be easy, but it seems to be the only step that can be taken in the direction we wish to go. Before it can reach the stage of actual formation, changes may be forced by the pressure of events; but the creation and successful operation of such a union would be a gain in itself and a portent of what may be possible elsewhere, say among the Scandinavian countries or in the Western Hemisphere.

If a disagreement with Mr. Jordan were to be recorded, it would be on his failure to develop more fully the relations between Central Union and the rest of the world. To many students, regionalism by itself is inadequate even as a next step. Some sort of world-wide organization is urged, which will have more strength than the League of Nations and with regional groups or union within the larger framework. But Mr. Jordan is probably wise in his approach. His present purpose is a limited one. In any case, something is imperative to bring together all or at any rate most of the countries he includes in his study. If at the same time Central Union can be made a part of a world organization or league or federation, so much the better. If that proves impossible, a limited union is a vast gain over the past and will lessen if not fully eliminate the strains in the area covered. As a proposal for Eastern Europe and as a method of approaching similar perplexities elsewhere, the idea of Central Union is to be heartily recommended for study. The recent break of relations between Turkey and Germany and the rapid advance of the Soviet Army means that both the Soviet Union and Turkey will powerfully affect any adjustments that are made.

University of Pennsylvania,
Wharton School of Finance and Commerce,
Philadelphia, Pa.,
August 10, 1944.

EUROPE SIMPLIFIED

BRITISH EMPIRE IN CLOSE ALLIANCE WITH U. S. A.

SCANDINAVIAN UNION

GERMAN FEDERATION

CENTRAL UNION

SOVIET UNION

LATIN LEAGUE

FIRST STEP

AMERICANS often wonder why Europe is split into many countries instead of forming a United States of Europe. This is due to historical tradition and to differences of language, custom and mental outlook. Another important reason which prohibits the establishment of a U.S.E.: European nations are unequal in size.

This has more bearing on the matter than might at first be thought. The smaller nations will not combine with the big ones, because they are afraid of being dominated. This fear has been justified by the behavior of Great Powers. As things now stand, only two countries on the Continent of Europe can claim the rank of great powers: Germany and Russia. The remaining nations, ranging in size from 42 millions (France) to 1 million inhabitants (Albania), do not want either of these great powers to become master of the continent—the more so as both of them are anti-democratic in tradition and current practice.

That is why a straightforward federation of the whole of Europe is not possible at the present moment, nor would it be likely to bring anything but misery and oppression to the smaller nations, which constitute—after all—the majority of the population of Europe. Obviously the division of Europe into more than twenty sovereign States, such as existed until 1939, cannot be continued indefinitely. Something will have to be done after the war to consolidate Europe and give it the peace and security without which there can be no peace for the rest of the world, especially for America.

The best solution would seem to be one dealing with the causes which prevent the federation of Europe: the excessive variety of political ambitions and the inequality of the various countries. By establishing regional federations the number of States in Europe could be reduced to six or seven, a great improvement on the existing situation and a step towards the consolidation of the entire Continent.

What could be the regional federations of Europe? One of them is already in existence. It is Russia.

Between Russia and Germany are eleven smaller countries, which could form a federation of their own—the Central Union.

Then there is Germany—a unit large enough in itself and that should not be allowed to absorb any smaller nations, which would be wiped out by German rule.

In the north there is Scandinavia, forming a distinct geographical and cultural unit.

In the west there are several possibilities: either a Britain federated with France and the Low Countries, leaving Italy, Spain and Portugal to form a Latin Union, or a larger Latin Union, including France, with Britain left alone as the metropolis of her Empire.

14

In either case, Europe would then be composed of only six States of approximately equal strength and size, none of which would risk annihilation by combining with others —as would have been the case with smaller nations absorbed individually by Great Powers. By far the most difficult task in this new organisation of Europe would be the foundation of the Central Union. The establishment of a Latin Union of only three or four nations would be relatively simpler. Yet none of the six States of that Europe of the near future would have greater importance for the peace and prosperity of the whole continent than the Central Union—because of its unique position between Russia and Germany.

That is why the present study is concerned with the Central Union, the creation of which is indispensable before any more comprehensive plans of federation in Europe can become feasible.

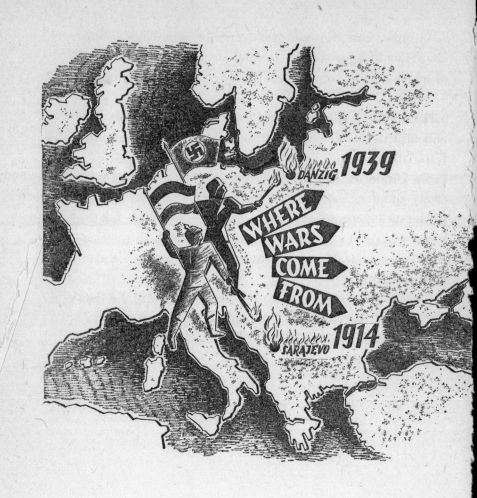

WHY?

ONE OF THE LEAST KNOWN PARTS of Europe is that which stretches from the Baltic in the north to the Adriatic and Ægean in the south, between Germany and Russia. It is notable, amongst other things, for the number of wars which started there. The superficial observer is apt to say: "Ah, those small countries squabbling again!" But the truth is that the wars which start in the Middle Zone of Europe are not due to the pugnacious instincts of the smaller nations. All the wars fought in that part of Europe were either openly started or secretly instigated by one of the Great Powers.

The Middle Zone is indispensable to any Power desiring the mastery of the Continent—and subsequently of the world. Its natural resources, its reserves of manpower, but most of all its key position make the Middle Zone the first objective of aggression for any ambitious continental dictator. Napoleon had to conquer the Middle Zone and so had Hitler. There is nothing to suggest that the list of dictators who want to make the Middle Zone a stage in their march to world power is finished.

Every time a controversy of some kind arises between any of the nations of the Middle Zone, it is exploited by

17

one or several Great Powers for their own ends. Since the two most powerful neighbors of the Middle Zone are Germany and Russia, they have invariably sought to promote their interests by backing one nation against another, or one faction within the same country against another. The result has usually been war.

The western powers—France and Britain—have so far give only scant attention to the Middle Zone. They have generally failed to realise that it is to a large extent one entity, a group of countries with many common features and identical interests. France tried at one time to consolidate a few of the nations of the Middle Zone, but her policy was not supported at that time by Britain, and French diplomacy took a narrow view of the whole matter. In consequence the nations of the Middle Zone were split and some of them accepted German leadership. Others offered stubborn and heroic resistance, but they were attacked one by one, and could not save their freedom. Now they are all under German domination: another unifying circumstance.

After the present war, France may be unable for some time to play a leading part in European affairs. The Middle Zone, ravaged by the enemy, will be facing the problem of reconstruction. Unless Britain and America give a strong lead and help the Middle Zone to achieve unity, that ill-fated region is bound to become the scene of a new war. Like all the other conflicts which started there, it may spread far and wide—perhaps across the world.

18

Split up and divided among ten different sovereign States, the Middle Zone can only be a potential cause of major disturbances—or the victim of one of the neighboring Great Powers. United in close co-operation with the great democracies, it can become an asset to world security and peace.

The local antagonism between the various nations can and should be settled once and for all by an impartial referee with no axe to grind and no common frontiers with any of the parties concerned.

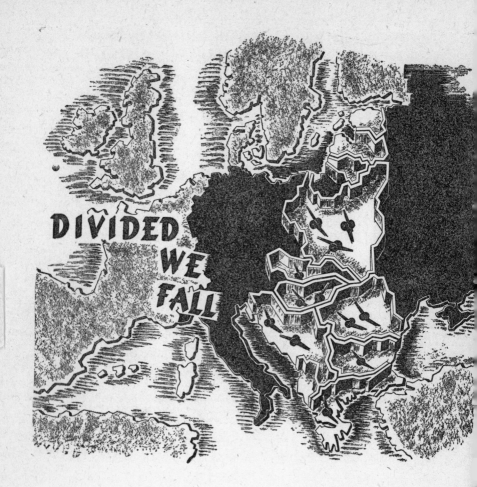

THE HUNTING GROUND OF AGGRESSORS

THE MIDDLE ZONE comprises the following countries, from north to south: the Baltic countries (Estonia and Latvia), Lithuania, Poland, Czecho-Slovakia, Hungary, Rumania, Yugoslavia, Bulgaria, Albania and Greece. In the period between 1918 and 1939, the Middle Zone was governed by eleven separate governments, each maintaining diplomatic representatives at the capitals of all the others. Every one of the eleven sovereign States had erected customs barriers and negotiated its own commercial agreements with the others. There were eleven separate Armies and Air Forces, to say nothing of the Navies of those nations which had any.

The largest single unit was Poland, with 35,000,000 inhabitants. When it was conquered by Germany the remaining countries became very easy prey. They were invaded one by one, while some surrendered and joined forces with Germany rather than be subdued by military occupation.

And yet the joint population of the eleven countries concerned was in 1939 about 115,000,000—far more than that of Germany. Their combined armies were quite strong, and they possessed considerable economic resources. The Middle Zone has many industries, and is on the whole a far more civilised region than is commonly supposed in the West.

The various local antagonisms were skilfully exploited by the Germans, who had a Fifth Column minority in every country. The vast area between the Baltic and the Mediterranean, bordered by Germany in the west and Russia in the east, was an amorphous mass of separate communities, without a co-ordinated policy or common ideals. This seems strange, since the interests of all the nations within the Zone are practically identical. None of them is strong enough to have any aggressive ambitions. They have all experienced foreign rule, and their one desire is to be free. The freedom of the nations of the Middle Zone is in no case seriously menaced by the mutual conflicts which arise between them from time to time. None of the Middle Zone nations is large enough to absorb another, did it even want to do so. The real danger can come only either from Germany in the west, or from Russia in the east. Even Italy should not be dangerous if Germany were not strong.

There has been a tendency among the nations of the Zone to seek the protection of Germany against Russia, or *vice versa*, thus providing both these powers with opportunities for intervention. As a rule the nations bordering on Germany prefer the protection and friendship of Russia, e.g. Czecho-Slovakia; while those bordering on Russia are inclined to accept German protection, e.g. Rumania. This tendency helped to split the Zone into many factions, thus reducing its ability to resist either of its two great neighbors.

Poland happens to be the only country in the Middle Zone which has *both Germany and Russia for neighbors.* This fact is very significant, for it makes that country inclined to keep a balance between these two powers and to submit to neither. Similar tendencies exist also in other countries, notably in Yugoslavia and Greece; but in Poland there are definite geographical reasons for non-submission to either German or Russian tutelage. Actually, however, the progress of military science has placed all the countries of the Zone in the same position as Poland, though some of the nations concerned have been slow to realise it.

A STRONGHOLD OF PEACE

THE EUROPEAN SITUATION in 1939 might have been very different from what it was, if Germany had been faced by one Federation of nearly 120 million inhabitants, instead of eleven small countries. The united military and economic resources of the nations of the Middle Zone were not inferior to those of Germany. Assisted by Britain and France, the nations of the Middle Zone could have resisted Germany successfully. In fact, the war would have probably never started at all.

It was impossible to expect the nations of Central Europe to unite in 1933 or 1936 simply because of the German danger. The consolidation could have been carried out only in 1918, when Europe was in the melting pot. As strict adherence to the principle of self-determination was the basis of the Versailles settlement, the establishment of a Central Union was not taken into consideration in 1918.

At the next Peace Conference, however, the situation will be very different. The nations concerned have already been unified to some extent, through belonging for several years to the same political and economic system—even though it was a hostile one. Just as Napoleon's conquest of the German States helped and hastened the unification of Germany, so

Hitler's conquest of Central Europe will assist its eventual consolidation.

The principle of self-determination is not to be lightly discarded. It must be respected in relations between the component nations of the Central Union. The internal administrative boundaries between the member States should conform as closely as possible to the boundaries of language and culture. It should be possible to apply the principle of self-determination quite strictly between the member nations, because considerations of military security or economic expediency will no longer have to be taken into account amongst them.

As to the external frontiers of the Union, however, the dominant principle must be political and economic security. The outside frontiers of the Union as a whole must be such as to make it a strong political and economic unit, capable of survival without outside assistance.

The establishment of the Union will certainly be viewed with disfavor by those Great Powers which have been in the habit of fishing in the troubled waters of Central Europe for imperialist profits and advantages. It will, on the other hand, be welcomed with the greatest satisfaction by those genuinely democratic and peaceful Powers which desire to maintain justice and peace in the world. They will find that, instead of being something of a liability, the Central European nations will become a valuable asset in the organisation of world peace. The Central Union will be powerful enough—at any rate after the period of initial organisation—to resist any aggression. It will also exert a steadying influence on the whole European situation, especially as it will be bound by ties of close understanding with the great democracies of the world. It is to be hoped that the Central Union may evolve a way of life modelled to some extent on the great democratic Union on the other side of the Atlantic—the United States of America.

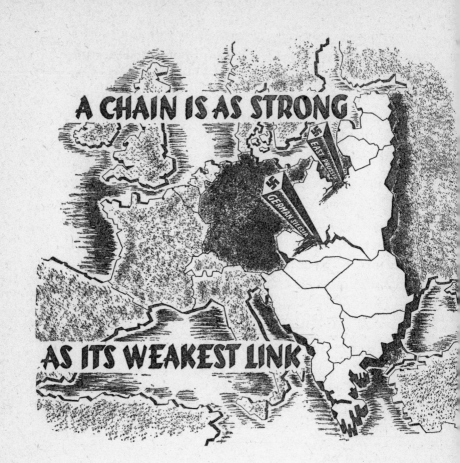

THE DANGER POINTS

It has been for several centuries the ambition of Germany
to break down the chain of free nations between the Baltic
and the Mediterranean. The Germans in their political advance applied methods similar to those of their military
campaigns: encirclement and pincer movements. Since
Prussia was the motive power of the German drive, the
most dangerous attacks were made in the north. East Prussia was founded by the Germans as an invasion base against
the Slavs. It was the northern arm of a huge pincer, of
which Silesia was the southern arm.

The German plan was to drive a wedge between western
and eastern Poland, thus splitting the country into two
and absorbing one part after the other. As to Silesia, it is
a wedge driven between the Poles and the Czechs. It has
always been clear to the Germans—if not to the nations
concerned—that Polish-Czech solidarity could form a powerful barrier against the German eastward expansion. That
is why Frederick the Great conquered Silesia, which is a
valuable strategic position for dividing the Slavs and as-
sisting their domination by the Germans. Later, Silesia
proved to be the repository of great natural wealth—coal
and iron—and it became one of Germany's arsenals.

It will be necessary to the interests of the Central Union to remove these two dangerous wedges. East Prussia has a large Polish population, so that only about one and a half million Germans will have to be repatriated to the Reich —a transfer of population on a scale that has become quite common in the course of the present war. As to Silesia, it also has a large Slav population, and the number of Germans who would have to return to the Fatherland would not be excessive. It would be, of course, intolerable to keep German minorities within the Union. The presence of such German minorities would be a cause of permanent unrest and possibly an excuse for war. For the same reason, the inclusion of Austria in the Central Union seems undesirable, for it would inevitably become a nucleus of German influence and interference. Austria may either remain independent, or join some kind of controlled German Federation—but that is an entirely separate problem.

The removal of the danger points of East Prussia and Silesia will shorten the western frontier of the Union by many hundred miles. It will also give it adequate access to the Baltic Sea.

It is quite possible that the relations between a chastised and re-educated Germany—perhaps in twenty years' time —and the Central Union may be peaceful and friendly. To achieve that objective, however, it will be necessary to establish conditions in which Germany can no longer think of attacking the nations of the Middle Zone. This requires two things: the consolidation of those nations into one

30

Union, and the establishment of a fairly straight and short frontier, without any German enclaves or excrescences.

Such a settlement, completed by the repatriation of all German minorities in the Middle Zone, will help the cause of a future friendly understanding with Germany far more than any half-measures leaving loopholes and opportunities for new aggression.

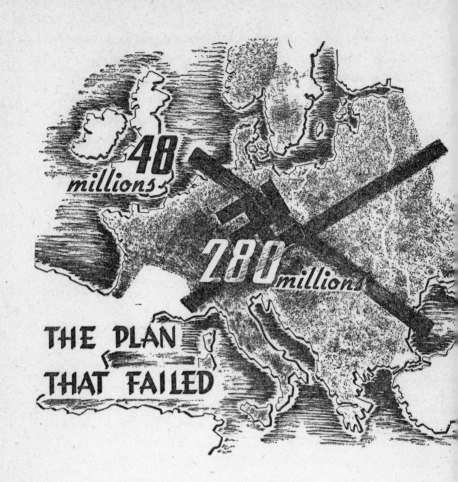

48 millions

280 millions

THE PLAN
THAT FAILED

PAN-GERMAN IMPERIALISM

IN THE PRESENT STATE of distribution of population and industrial power, Europe is still the dominant continent of the world. This may have changed in fifty years' time, but we are concerned with the present. It is difficult to imagine —in terms of technical possibilities—a conquest of the world starting from Asia or America, whereas a conquest of the world starting from Europe has narrowly missed success.

To conquer the world with Europe as starting point, one has to master the entire continent first. The initial stage is traditionally and inevitably the occupation of the Middle Zone, that inner core of the European continent. It is possible to visualize a plan of world hegemony overlooking countries like Norway, Sweden or Spain, but there are regions which have to be conquered before any further steps can be taken. These regions are: Western Europe, viz., Britain, France and the Low Countries; and the Middle Zone.

Working out their plan of world conquest logically and relentlessly, the Germans were fully aware of these facts and they began both their world wars with the occupation of the Middle Zone. Its resources are considerable: coal

33

and iron in Poland and Czecho-Slovakia, oil in Rumania and Poland, bauxite and copper in Yugoslavia, agricultural products throughout the Zone. The greatest wealth of the Middle Zone, however, is its manpower. There are very few comparable reservoirs of labor in the world: North America, Western Europe, Russia, Japan, Germany. Each of these concentrations of manpower is also a centre of political forces. China and India, though they have immense populations, cannot be compared with Central Europe, inhabited by nations which have shared in the achievements of western civilization since its very inception. It is remarkable that the mass of 120 million Central Europeans, constituting one of the greatest reservoirs of skilled labor in the world, has not yet formed its own political organization.

In the meantime, the huge population of Central Europe —a mass of well-educated and highly intelligent people— can be put at the service of any power that conquers the Middle Zone. No doubt the people of the Middle Zone can achieve far more working freely for their own ideals than they can do working under coercion for alien interests. Nevertheless, they are, even as mere slaves, one of the greatest labor forces in the world.

That is why Germany wanted to lay the foundations of her world empire in the Middle Zone. Her plan is bound to fail, even though she still holds the key territories. It will fail mainly because she conquered the Middle Zone by force. If Germany had managed to enlist the co-operation of the Middle Zone, without starting a world war in the process, she would have had within ten years at her disposal a force unequalled in the world. She could then have launched her attack and probably would have won against all comers. But by having to fight for the Middle Zone, Germany gave away her plans and lost her chance.

The formula for world conquest, revised in the light of Hitler's experience, is this: take possession of the Middle Zone without starting a general war, establish yourself firmly there without alarming your possible opponents, and then strike when you are ready. That, incidentally, was Hitler's original plan, upset by the "unreasonable" attitude of nations like Poland, Yugoslavia and Greece. They were prepared to fight against any odds. No sensible world empire-planner could have foreseen such folly! It made all the difference.

The next player bidding for the same stake will certainly remember Hitler's lesson and will do his utmost to take by stealth those vantage points without which he cannot start the real game.

48 millions

280 millions

THE PLAN
THAT WILL FAIL

IMPERIALISM OF THE PANSLAV DOCTRINE

THE ONLY OTHER IMPERIALISM which might have a direct interest in the Middle Zone is that of the Slavs. It is not the intention of the writer to suggest that such an imperialism exists, but in a scientific survey of all the possible—even though perhaps hypothetical—contingencies, it is difficult to overlook this alternative.

Catherine the Great had ideas on the subject of the Middle Zone which were not unlike those of Frederick the Great. Since they were contemporaries, neither of the two monarchs could fully realise his plans, which more or less cancelled each other.

If there should be at any time a return to imperialist tradition in Russia, the idea of a Middle Zone united under Russian "leadership" might certainly have a strong appeal. The old Panslav doctrine was based on the same principle. All the Slav nations except Russia happen to live in the Middle Zone, so that Panslavism amounts to advocating the incorporation of the Zone by the largest of all Slav powers.

In fact the idea of a Panslavism, involving the creation of a vast bloc between Germany and the Pacific, has potentialities which the German plan of *Mitteleuropa* never possessed. There are more Slavs than there are Germans and their birth-rate is much higher. On the other hand, there are basic differences between the Western Slavs of the Middle Zone and the Russians.

So far the Slavs have seemed, on the whole, to be more peacefully disposed than most other races. It is difficult to forecast what might happen if the Slavs felt—for the first time in history—real power in their hands. The situation is complicated by the fact that the Russians, though speaking a Slav language, have a strong dose of Asiatic blood in their veins.

The idea of a giant State, including Russia and all the countries of the Middle Zone, possibly others as well, may appear attractive to some people—notably members of the larger Slav nations. Other countries might take a different view of the matter. The germ of imperialism is ever dormant in human nature, and it takes centuries to learn to wield power without abusing it.

The power at the command of whoever might control the Pan-Slav Empire—or Greater Russia, which it would amount to—would be greater than that of any other ruler of modern times. It would be definitely superior to that of a German dictator controlling the Middle Zone. Such powers, if used for good, could achieve magnificent results. Turned to evil ends, it could cause untold damage. Unfortunately men are seldom in agreement as to what is good and what is evil.

As to the nations of the Middle Zone, their idea of good is based on the Western, Christian and democratic principle of individual and national freedom. They are not attracted by the notion of accomplishing gigantic political feats at the cost of oceans of sweat and blood. Grandiose visions of world empires leave them cold—and very uneasy. A time may come when a World State will be possible—but it seems far away. The era of small sovereign States is over, but it might be a serious error to try to jump the intermediary period of large regional federations and establish huge intercontinental States at once. Such a premature step would strengthen the forces of totalitarian nationalism, instead of leading towards their gradual dissolution. It would also inevitably result in a world war for hegemony over the whole earth.

That is why the creation of a Pan-Slav Empire is neither likely, nor particularly desirable at the present stage of world evolution.

THE PLAN THAT MUST NOT FAIL

SECURITY WITHOUT IMPERIALISM

PAN-GERMANISM is a doctrine which implies the idea of domination by its very name. The idea of a Central European Union, on the other hand, is not based on any racial scheme nor does it aim at imperialist expansion. Including all the smaller countries of Central Europe, the Union would be unable for a long time to achieve that uniformity of language, custom and thought which is the characteristic feature of all totalitarian and imperialist States. The Union could never become a menace to its neighbors, because its only two neighbors are the two strongest powers of the Continent, which have nothing to fear from a peaceful federation of small nations—while the reverse may sometimes be the case.

The defensive strength of the Central Union, however, would be sufficient to guarantee its security.

From the point of view of European and world peace, the importance of the Central Union would be twofold: (1) It would collaborate actively with the democratic and peaceful powers, (2) by its very existence, the Central Union would prevent any would-be conqueror from seizing the most vital strategic area in Europe.

41

Most of the nations of the Middle Zone have hitherto been living either in poverty or, at any rate, at a much lower standard than that of Western Europe. They were in consequence bad customers and the Middle Zone did not share in world trade to any great extent. This situation was detrimental to the nations concerned and to world trade in general.

The reason for the economic under-development of most countries in the Middle Zone was simple: they had not enjoyed freedom in the XIXth century and even when they became independent, there was no security, and the energy of each nation was absorbed by defence preparations, instead of being turned to constructive work.

If the Middle Zone were included in a Pan-German Empire, it is to be feared that such a vast State might establish complete autarchy and become self-sufficient. This could be achieved at the cost of keeping down the standard of living and of crippling world trade by the elimination of a market of several hundred million customers.

The Central Union, on the contrary, could not entertain ideas of totalitarian economy, and it would certainly trade with the outside world as much as possible. It could trade both with its immediate neighbors—unless they persisted in their autarchic policies—and with the rest of the world, thanks to its Baltic and Mediterranean ports. There is no doubt that the joint foreign trade of the Union could greatly exceed the combined turnover of the member countries at the time when they pursued independent and often contradictory commercial policies. Immense opportunities for business enterprise would be opened in the Middle Zone.

The nations of the Middle Zone, even those which temporarily collaborate with Hitler, do not desire to belong to either a Pan-German or a Pan-Slav Empire. They want freedom, but they are beginning to realize that they cannot have it unless they surrender a part of their sovereignty to save the rest. Any plan based on the idea of the "leadership" of a Great Power with direct interests in the Middle Zone is unacceptable to the free nations of Central Europe. The enforcement of such a plan could result only in unrest and dissatisfaction, ultimately in a new war. It seems better, therefore, to choose the middle way and leave the nations of the Middle Zone free, giving them an organization which could make of that part of Europe a solid entity, capable of effective co-operation with other peace-loving nations.

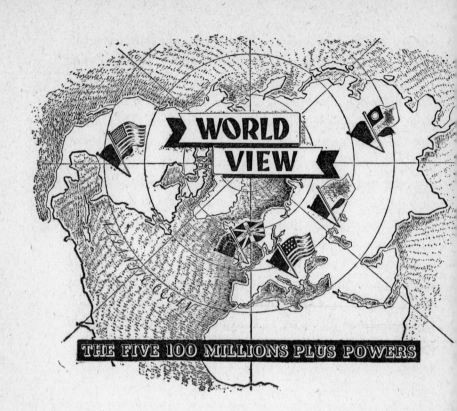

WORLD
VIEW

THE FIVE 100 MILLIONS PLUS POWERS

DEMOCRACY DOMINANT

THERE IS NO WORD more flagrantly abused than "democracy." A sincere writer using that term should, therefore, give his own definition of its meaning. I do not propose to indulge in legal and philosophical dissertations. Most of us believe, rightly or wrongly, that democracy is a form of government which safeguards the individual against the tyranny of the all-powerful State; which recognizes freedom of speech and of the Press; which admits the existence of more than one party and does not give precedence or privilege to any party, group or class; which protects the freedom of the courts and does not tolerate imprisonment on any ground other than a criminal offence, certainly not on suspicion of political non-conformity; which gives equal treatment to all creeds and races; which admits the possibility of a change of government by legal means and does not establish dictators who can only be removed by revolution; which respects human dignity and does not enforce the regimentation of private lives; which gives equal opportunity to all, without discriminating against any class— either low or high.

This list could be lengthened, but these few examples may have been sufficient to outline a common man's idea

45

of democracy considered as a practical way of life, not as an abstract theory.

The great majority of the people of the Middle Zone, although they have not always enjoyed the benefits of democracy, ardently desire to live as free men and women. They realize that they can achieve genuine personal freedom and democratic government only if their countries remain independent—particularly from any intervention of the totalitarian powers.

It is too early to foresee the constitutional form of the Central Union—whether it would be a Confederation; a very close alliance of powers with a common foreign, defense and economic policy, or some other kind of organization. The internal constitutions of the component countries may not be identical—some countries may desire to remain monarchies, others republics. But it would be essential to adopt a basic Charter of Civic Rights, to be adopted by every nation in the Union. It should be a Charter guaranteeing those rights of free men without which genuine democracy is unthinkable.

There are not many countries in the world where the system of government even approaches the ideal of true democracy. Very few of them are great powers. And yet it is an inescapable fact that unless the democratic powers are stronger than those which are not, democracy and human freedom will perish from the earth. The appearance on the map of a new democratic country, especially one which might soon claim the rank of a great power, would be a fact of tremendous importance for the world which we are accustomed to call the world of western civilization.

Some of the nations of the Middle Zone have had an admittedly scant experience of democracy. But this region, taken as a whole, has come at times nearer to true democratic freedom than either its western or its eastern neighbor. It is obvious that democratic government is more easily established and worked in small countries than in large ones. Since the member nations of the Union would presumably keep their independence in home affairs, they would have far better opportunities for evolving a genuine democracy than they could ever have as part of a giant Empire. The older democracies, notably those of the English-speaking nations, would have an interest in promoting democratic practice in the Central Union, for they have a greater stake than anyone else in maintaining the supremacy of democratic ideals in the world.

THE ONLY MEANS OF SURVIVAL

THE ERA of small countries seems to be over. The progress of the science of war, apart from other things, makes it impossible for a small country to defend its independence. A hundred years ago ten small countries, each contributing, say, 25,000 men, could build a common force as strong as the 250,000 army of a Great Power. To-day, unless the types of aircraft and tanks are uniform and unless their *performance is sufficiently high*, numbers no longer matter. Technical efficiency has a tremendous importance and no small country can possibly design and produce machines —whether for war or peace—which could keep pace with the machines designed by the research staffs of bigger and wealthier countries.

That is why ten separate armies totalling four or five million men do not actually have the fighting strength which that figure might suggest. In fact their joint strength is scarcely greater than that of the strongest individual army among them.

There are also other economic and political reasons which make it difficult for a small country to survive, unless it happens to be situated in a remote and sheltered part of the world. That is certainly not the case of the Middle Zone

49

of Europe, exposed as it is to greater outside pressure than any other region in the world.

It is, therefore, imperative for such countries to unite, unless they are prepared to forfeit their freedom and their very existence. It was rather fortunate for the nations of the Middle Zone that they were dominated by foreign powers during a period of relative liberalism, which extended even to the Ottoman Empire. It is clear that if the Middle Zone were occupied now, for a period of twenty years or more, by a totalitarian power, the subject nations could no longer emerge almost unscathed, as they did before. They would risk extermination or disintegration by such means as the deportation of millions of people to remote parts of the world. If the nations of the Middle Zone should lose their freedom now, they would lose it for ever. They would be wiped out and no revolution staged thirty or forty years later could save them, for they would no longer exist— except as crippled carcasses, doomed to prolonged agony and death.

This is a monstrous prospect—not only for the nations concerned, for such deeds invite repetition—and one which compels prompt action. Viewed in the perspective of such a fate as the alternative to union, all the antagonisms among the nations of the Middle Zone are reduced to their true puny proportions.

Although there have been many bitter feuds between the nations of the Middle Zone, none of them menaced seriously the independence of any of the countries concerned.

They were territorial disputes concerning border districts, but in no case did one of the smaller nations claim the entire territory or even half the territory of another.

The conflicts of the smaller nations within the Middle Zone with the neighboring great powers have always had an altogether different character: the latter threatened the smaller countries with complete loss of independence. Sometimes the initial claim did not embrace at first the whole territory of the smaller country, but the menace of complete absorption has always loomed behind every demand, however moderate it might have appeared at first.

That is why the countries of the Middle Zone can afford to be conciliatory and generous in settling their mutual disputes, but must be firm in resisting the claims of the neighboring great powers, known for their insatiable appetites.

KEYSTONE OF THE ARCH

"THE KEYSTONE of the arch" was Napoleon's description of the position of Poland in the European structure. It is probably more true to-day than it was 150 years ago.

Poland happens to be the largest nation in the Middle Zone. It had in 1939 a population of 35,000,000, while the next largest country, Rumania, had 20,000,000, and Czecho-Slovakia 15,000,000. It is true that the figure of 35,000,000 includes various national minorities, but even if we take as a basis of comparison national groups the Poles remain by far the largest nation in the Middle Zone: there are 27,-000,000 of them.

The geographical position of Poland is of the utmost political and strategic importance. It is the only country in the Middle Zone to have both Germany and Russia for neighbors. It is, in other words, the thinnest part of the Zone. If it should break down the rest will inevitably collapse—as recent events have proved.

It is obvious that Poland alone, isolated from the other nations of the Middle Zone, notably from its southern, Danubian neighbors, could not survive for long. But it is equally clear that the other countries of the Middle Zone could not hope to keep their freedom unless they are in

53

close collaboration with an independent Poland—not a mutilated puppet State in the valley of the Vistula.

As to Lithuania, it is a country which had been united with Poland for many centuries, when kings of Lithuanian blood sat on the Cracow throne. The relationship between Poland and Lithuania was almost exactly the same as between England and Scotland—except that the Union had been achieved much earlier (XIVth century). The Polish language and culture were adopted in Lithuania, while the part played by Lithuanians in the Polish Commonwealth was similar to that which Scotsmen are playing in the British Empire. Many of the greatest Polish leaders were Lithuanians by origin—men like Mickiewicz, the national poet, or Pilsudski, the soldier-statesman.

During the war of 1914–18 Lithuania was occupied by the Germans, together with the rest of the Polish Commonwealth. Faithful to their policy of dividing the smaller nations and setting them against each other, the Germans instigated anti-Polish tendencies in Lithuania. They also encouraged Lithuanian claims to Wilno, which used to be the capital of Lithuania in the Middle Ages, when Lithuanian Princes ruled territories inhabited by White Ruthenians, and extending far beyond the boundaries of Lithuania proper.

There is no doubt, however, that the essential identity of interests between Poland and Lithuania, assisted by common tradition, will enable the two brother nations to

54

revive their ancient union, within the broader framework of the Central Union.

The events of recent years prove that Lithuania cannot remain independent unless Poland is also free. The Wilno dispute appears insignificant when the very existence of both nations is at stake, and certainly some solution can be found when such grave matters are in the balance. It does not really matter in what manner the Wilno problem will be solved, provided Poland and Lithuania establish complete harmony, forgetting the German intrigues which have been disturbing it in recent years.

There are many Lithuanians in the north-eastern corner of East Prussia, just as there are many Poles in the southern part of the German invasion base. The liquidation of that outpost of Teutonic imperialism is vital for the entire Union. Lithuania should get the part inhabited by her people, while the rest should go to Poland.

THE INDUSTRIAL BACKBONE

OF ALL THE COUNTRIES of the Middle Zone, Czecho-Slovakia is economically the most advanced. It is also one of the most democratic. The connection between these two features is obvious.

Czecho-Slovakia holds the central position in the Middle Zone. The shape of that country, formed for the first time in history at Versailles in 1919, is not favorable from the point of view of security. Bohemia—the main part of Czecho-Slovakia—is encircled by Austria in the south and by the German wedge of Silesia in the north. Czecho-Slovakia was menaced by Germany from the very beginning of its existence and the fact influenced its policy. Since Czecho-Slovakia has no common frontier with Russia, it has usually been pro-Russian.

Unlike some other nations in the Middle Zone, Czecho-Slovakia never had any illusions as to the practical possibilities of defending her independence alone. She was, therefore, inclined to accept the protection of a stronger power —France or Russia. The events of 1938–39 proved that Czecho-Slovak reliance on outside help erred on the side of optimism. The consequent disappointment caused some justifiable bitterness.

Of all these eleven nations only the Czechs have shown a real desire of association with the Soviets.

Even the union of Poland with Bohemia and Slovakia would form a strong State, with far better chances of survival than either country could ever have separately. If such a union had existed before 1938, Hitler would have been faced by a State of 50,000,000 inhabitants, with the arms of Skoda and the manpower of Poland.

Such a union is all the more desirable as the Polish, Slovak and Czech languages are very similar and the culture of the three nations has many common elements, while the differing features of their character are complementary: e.g., Polish boldness and Czech organizing ability. But even a Western-Slav State of 50 millions would not be strong enough to withstand the tremendous political pressure on the Middle Zone. Only a broad and comprehensive solution—the Central Union—can hope to be permanent. All the countries of the Middle Zone without exception should unite—for only then can they become an asset to their Western European allies, instead of being a liability.

In the interest of the Central Union as a whole, the Silesian wedge should be lopped off, allowing a broader point of contact between Poland and Czecho-Slovakia. As to the Sudeten Germans, they should be repatriated to the Reich, for it would be suicidal to tolerate German minori-

58

ties within the Union. That is why the inclusion of Austria is not desirable.

The Cieszyn frontier controversy between Poland and Czecho-Slovakia is one of those secondary problems which cannot be allowed to become an obstacle to the realization of a great work of peace.

Thanks to its industrial equipment, Czecho-Slovakia would probably benefit economically from the establishment of the Central Union more than almost any other member State. Politically, there is no doubt that membership in a federation of free and democratic nations would be far safer than dependence on a foreign power.

HUNGARY and
RUMANIA
POLAND
CZECHOSLOVAKIA
MISCOLC
BUDAPEST
10 million inhabitants
ORADEA
NAGY KANIZSA
CERNAUTI
JASSY
20 million inhabitants
GALATZ
BUCHAREST
YUGOSLAVIA
BULGARIA

FRIENDS OR FOES?

THE RECORD of the governments of Hungary and Rumania in the present war—or for that matter in the last one—cannot inspire their countrymen with particular pride. If, however, some people frantically persist in claiming that there are "good Germans," surely we may admit the existence of good Hungarians and Rumanians.

Hungary is an old nation, perhaps somewhat inclined to live in the past, but not lacking in contemporary talent. Rumania is a relatively new nation.

They have both given way to German pressure and become the tools of Hitler. It would be difficult to condemn them for acting as they have done, for their position was extremely precarious and no one has the right to expect of any man or nation the spirit of selfless sacrifice displayed in Poland, Yugoslavia and Greece. Heroism cannot be looked upon as a duty, for it would then no longer be sublime.

The Hungarians are proud and they bitterly resented their treatment after the last war. It would be a major blunder to continue treating them as enemies. Such generosity towards a nation capable of ferocious revenge, like Germany, would be reckless, but in dealing with Hungary the victors can afford to be generous without taking risks.

Owing to its geographical position, Hungary is indispensable to the Central Union—and there can be no subject and master nations within that Union. That alone indicates a line of policy with regard to the Hungarian question. All the frontier disputes between Hungary and its neighbors should be definitely settled, with transfers of population where necessary. The resulting Hungary would probably be a compromise between the territory of 1919 and the position of 1942.

The idea of a "Danubian Federation," propounded on many occasions, may be sound in principle, but it is not and never can be a complete solution of the problem. A union of the Danubian countries alone, excluding the rest of the Middle Zone, would be quite inadequate to ensure peace in that part of Europe without outside help.

As to Rumania, it is a relatively new nation and its political evolution is not yet very far advanced. The potential wealth of the country, however, is considerable. So far it has been exploited mainly by foreign interests, and the economic structure of the country has in consequence remained rudimentary. There seems to be no reason why Rumania, as a member of an international organization guaranteeing her security, could not become a prosperous democratic country.

The frontier disputes between Rumania and her neighbors should be definitely settled. like those of Hungary. In delimiting the internal boundaries between members of the Union, it would be advisable to adhere to the ethno-

62

graphical principle, with exchanges of population in enclaves.

It is probable and indeed desirable that there should be a gradual merging of the nationalities of the Union, but no greater error could be made than to try to accelerate that process, which must be entirely natural and voluntary. Within less than a century, we shall witness the birth of a new national consciousness—that of the Central Europeans, which will not exclude regional patriotism. This new, wider patriotism will arise if the Union becomes a fact. Otherwise the people of the Middle Zone will be forced to become Germans or Russians, or both.

THE SOUTHERN SLAVS

IN THE COURSE of the present war few nations have gone through more vicissitudes than Yugoslavia. The courage displayed by the Yugoslavs at the decisive moment was magnificent and incidentally it proved that no nation can be wholly absolved from the misdeeds of its rulers, for most bad governments can be overthrown if the will is there.

The epic campaign of General Mihailovic confirmed once again the high reputation of the Yugoslavs for patriotism and courage. The intrigues carried on against that national leader give a measure of the difficulties which may be encountered in post-war reconstruction. There are interests desiring the maximum disruption in Central Europe and determined to promote chaos in order to further their own imperialist aims. If these attempts are not frustrated, the Middle Zone and then the rest of Europe may become the scene of a new war, more savage than the present one. If the nations of the Middle Zone establish a firm solidarity, assisted by peace-loving powers not interested in imperialist expansion, the danger may be averted.

After their recent experience, the Yugoslavs will certainly have realized that the survival of their country cannot be assured without the closest association with their neighbors. Yugoslavia has already concluded with Greece a pact which seems to be the forerunner of some kind of union between these two countries. It is the only pact of its kind between two nations of the Middle Zone, apart from the Polish-Czecho-Slovak agreement. It is obvious, however, that even Yugoslavia and Greece together could not safeguard their freedom against aggression. The idea of collaboration with Bulgaria or Hungary may be distasteful to the Yugoslavs, whose relations with Bulgarians and Hungarians have seldom been very pleasant.

It would be difficult for Yugoslavia to associate with her old opponents in a simple Balkan Union, because she would be afraid of hostile machinations by some of her neighbors. In a large Central Union, the situation would be different, for links of friendship have always existed between the Yugoslavs, Czechs and Poles.

Long before armed aggression, German economic penetration in the Balkans nearly robbed some countries of their independence and virtually turned them into German colonies. Within the Union every country will be assigned its economic part, fitting into a plan embracing the whole Middle Zone. Countries like Yugoslavia particularly will benefit by such arrangement, for they will no longer have to struggle against foreign economic domination, paving the way for conquest. The Central Union will be able to deal on equal terms with any country, without submitting to the pressure—sometimes amounting to blackmail—which used to be the lot of smaller countries before 1939.

As to Albania, it is far too small to exist in modern conditions as a sovereign State. Membership in the Union will give to such small countries far better opportunities for development and progress than they could ever get as clients of Great Powers. Cultural autonomy will be the rule throughout the Union and local languages will continue to be used, so that the small nations will not be threatened by the annihilation which is the usual outcome of their relations with rapacious great powers.

LAND OF HEROES AND BAD BOY
OF THE BALKANS

THESE TWO COUNTRIES are bracketed together by way of
contrast and not because of any affinity. Greece, situated
at the southern end of the Middle Zone, has displayed in
the present war, as before, remarkable courage and patriotism. She can become a great asset to the Central Union,
for she possesses those qualities of idealism and breadth
of vision which are more necessary than anything else to
overcome prejudice and build great nations.

Membership in the Union will be highly beneficial to
Greece. It will give her greater security than could be ob-
tained by any bilateral pacts with other Balkan nations,
without loss of the guarantees which Greece may obtain
from the western powers. Economically, Greece will become one of the principal southern doorways of the whole
Union. Salonica will be one of the main ports of the Union,
with commercial opportunities it has never yet known.

The question of a Federal Navy and Merchant Marine
will have to be settled together with many other relevant
problems. It may be possible to have a Union flag (which
need not be that used on the cover of the present book) or
to maintain the flags of the member nations. In any case
it is obvious that the association of seafaring and purely

69

continental nations within one political body will bring mutual benefits to all. If there should be a Union Navy and Merchant Fleet in the Mediterranean, the Greeks—who are probably the only traditionally seafaring nation in the Middle Zone—would have an important part to play. Other nations might also develop navigating talent—as the Poles did after recovering their access to the sea in 1920.

The commercial ability of the Greeks, their gift for languages and general mental alertness, would find a rich field of opportunity in the Middle Zone, hitherto barred by tariff frontiers.

As to Bulgaria, it is a somewhat backward country, which does not seem to possess a true spirit of independence and has invariably become the tool of foreign powers. If the Bulgarians could surrender their independence to an alien great power without many qualms, they should find it easy to accept the slight limitations of sovereignty within the Union. At an early stage Bulgaria may not play a leading part in directing the affairs of the Union, but there is no doubt that it can eventually become a fully democratic and civilized country. Nothing could contribute to it more than a friendly association with nations which have reached a higher standard of culture and yet have certain common interests with Bulgaria. There will be no domination or "leadership" within the Union, but it is inevitable that the more highly-evolved nations will set a political and cultural standard which the less advanced nations will naturally try to emulate.

The frontier problems of Bulgaria are particularly delicate. To give full satisfaction to Bulgarian claims would be grossly unfair to other nations. To penalize Bulgaria excessively might be unwise, for nations with a justified grievance do not make good allies, still less members of a federation. The main thing is to strike a compromise and leave no national minorities on either side.

In any case, the general tendency of the Union will be towards the eventual blurring of national boundaries. In the early stages, however, it would not be practicable to dispense with frontiers altogether. They should be no more than administrative lines of demarcation, without customs or passport control. Their importance will gradually decrease, until even Bulgarians will no longer draw knives on approaching a frontier.

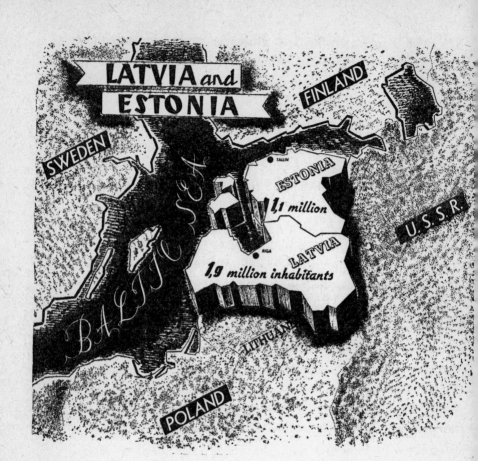

TEST FOR DEMOCRACY

THE TWO BALTIC COUNTRIES, Latvia and Estonia, belong geographically and politically to the Middle Zone, forming its northern extremity. They existed between 1920 and 1940 as fully sovereign States, but few Latvians or Estonians had any illusions about the permanence of their freedom. There was some talk of a "Baltic Union," but it is obvious that such a union would still be a very small State, unable to resist aggression.

From the point of view of international law, the Baltic countries are still independent, for territorial changes carried out by violence are never recognised by law, even if they masquerade as "legal acts," supported by "popular votes" held under foreign military occupation. It is a similar principle to that which denies any value to a document whereby a householder might have signed away all his silver to a burglar holding him at the point of a revolver. Even duly sealed and witnessed, such a document could not have any legal value—at any rate in the Western civilized world.

Three alternatives are open to the Baltic countries: to join a Scandinavian Union, together with Finland; to join the Central Union; or to join the Soviet Union. The fourth:

73

independence and isolation, could not last long and need not seriously be considered.

The first alternative might be attractive, but there is nothing to suggest that the Scandinavian nations desire association with the Baltic countries.

As to the Central Union, it can exist and prosper without the Baltic countries, but it would no doubt welcome them as members if they applied to join.

The Soviet Union also can exist and prosper without the Baltic countries, which are insignificant compared to the vast spaces of Russia. There is, however, some ground for believing that the Soviet Union, unlike Scandinavia, might not turn down an application from Latvia and Estonia for membership of the U.S.S.R.

The question remains open. It is not a particularly important problem from a purely political or economic point of view, for the countries concerned are small and have no riches. Its importance lies in the principles involved. Latvia and Estonia are small, weak nations, which cannot defend their rights with armed force. They are, on the other hand, civilized nations, which have many achievements to their credit and have proved themselves worthy of freedom.

Callous indifference to the fate of these two small and relatively democratic nations would be a most alarming symptom for the future of Europe. It would amount to the acknowledgment of the totalitarian principle of brute force as the only criterion of a nation's right to live.

It seems that the decision should be left to the people

concerned, who could state their will by plebiscite. It might be useful to state the requisites for a genuine and fair plebiscite: (1) The plebiscite territory should be under the effective control of a power neutral in the dispute, but strong enough to be respected, for several months before the poll. (2) The territory should be quite free of any troops or police, either uniformed or secret, of any of the powers interested in the outcome of the vote. (3) The vote should be strictly secret and the poll supervised by powers neutral to the dispute. (4) Strong measures should be taken to avoid intimidation—notably threats to the life and property of those casting their votes for what may turn out to be the losing side. (5) Only persons born in the territory should have the vote, including persons who have emigrated, but want to return. Recent residents should not vote. (6) The press and propaganda machinery should be internationally controlled, to prevent bribery and corruption.

Such a method might be applied to the Baltic countries. Democracy should not shirk from a test of the principles on which it must depend for its survival.

NO NEED FOR IMPERIALISM

CENTRAL UNION—THE FRIEND OF RUSSIA

IT GOES WITHOUT SAYING that the attitude of Russia towards the Central Union is of paramount importance. It can be stated categorically that whilst not one of the States comprising this Union has any desire to be incorporated into Russia, each of them individually, and all of them collectively, if incorporated within the Central Union, would desire to remain on the best possible terms with their great neighbor.

In the political field there should be a close community of interests. Both are equally interested in maintaining peace in Central Europe and preventing a resurgence of German nationalism which would eventually result in World War No. 3. For the first time in her history Russia would have between her and the west, from which danger has always threatened, a strong, united State which linked in treaty relationship with Great Britain, like Russia itself, could nip in the bud any new attempt by Germany at world domination.

Economically, anything which can raise the standard of living in Eastern Europe from its present desperately low level must benefit Russia, by increasing the value of trade between the two countries.

It would, however, be idle to deny that some Poles, remembering that Russia participated in all partitions of Poland, fear that she may wish to push her frontier westward to include parts of Poland and the three Baltic Republics of Latvia, Estonia and Lithuania. There are, surely, three answers to any such misgivings. The first that Russia has signed the Atlantic Charter, thereby solemnly renouncing any ideas of territorial aggrandisement. Russia would not wish to forfeit the goodwill of the U.S.A. and the British Commonwealth. She would certainly do so if, as a result of a war in which the whole world has united against aggression, she incorporated within her own boundaries any free peoples who wished to remain independent and were fully capable of so doing.

The second answer is that there could be no possible excuse for such action. The U.S.S.R. is the largest single contiguous block of territory within the same political system. She has ample resources both in raw materials and population to develop her standard of living to the highest possible level. A glance at the map which shows the enormous extent and the potential wealth of Russia in Europe and Asia should satisfy anyone that Russia certainly has no need of any part of the small countries adjoining her western frontier.

The third reason why Russian expansion should not be feared is that the creation of a strong Central Union should remove for ever the one legitimate excuse for such expansion, namely the fear of attack from Germany. As to the

78

possibility of the Central Union's being a menace to Russia herself, the question has only to be put in order to see its utter absurdity.

For these reasons it is to be hoped that Russia will support the idea of the Central Union. For the first time in modern history there is an opportunity, by the creation of this Union, to solve one of the most difficult problems of Europe. Russia would benefit by that solution no less than the peoples of the eleven countries concerned.

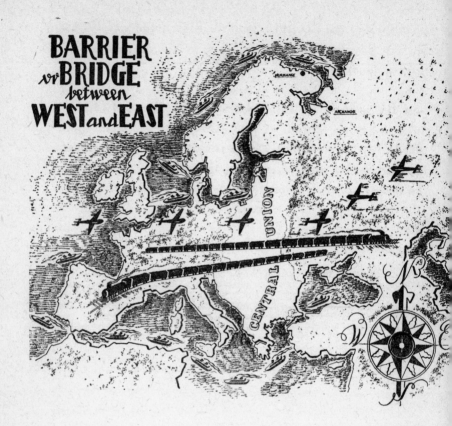

RUSSIAN DOORWAYS TO THE WORLD

IT IS SOMETIMES SUGGESTED by the more ardent partisans of Russia that any kind of international co-operation in Central Europe is undesirable, because it might amount to the formation of a *"cordon sanitaire"* alleged to divide Russia from Europe. The term is calculated to arouse suspicion and disgust—it was coined by a French statesman after the last war.

It would admittedly be deplorable if the Central Union should in any way alienate Russia from Europe, or erect any barrier between that country and Western Europe. There can be no question at all of a geographical isolation of Russia, which has ports in the Arctic, Baltic and Black Seas.

The territory of the Central Union would be open, of course, to all kinds of traffic between Europe and Russia— by rail, road and air on the largest possible scale. It is difficult to see how the formation of the Central Union can adversely affect the traffic between West and East. On the contrary, a federal organization of transport could achieve great improvement on the 1939 conditions. The number of frontiers would be reduced. For instance, a Russian travelling from Moscow to Rome in 1938 had to cross five or six international frontiers, while after the establishment of the Union he would have only two frontiers to cross.

It is obvious that the Central Union can in no way impede the commercial or cultural relations between Russia and Europe, but may render them easier. This seems to suggest that the vehement critics of Central European Federation have other objections at the back of their minds. They may feel that a democratic federation in the Middle Zone might become an obstacle to the westward expansion of Russia. Their misgivings are, however, unjustified, since the Russian government has declared solemnly and on many occasions that it desires no territorial aggrandisement and that it does not propose to spread abroad its particular methods of government.

During the last twenty-five years Russia has to some extent been isolated from Europe, but it would be unfair to blame for it any country other than Russia herself. For reasons of home policy, the Russian government did not allow its nationals to travel abroad, except on important official business. It also controlled closely the foreign tourist traffic to Russia.

A change of this policy could contribute to a genuine understanding and friendship between Russia and other nations. It is to be hoped that after the war we shall see Russians travelling all over Europe in thousands and that travel in Russia will become as free and easy for foreigners as it is in France or Britain.

Trade with Russia could be developed with mutual bene-

82

fit. As to cultural relations, the possibilities are immense. Everything depends on freedom of travel, with as few passport, visa and currency restrictions as possible. No one in Europe will be more eager to entertain the closest relations with Russia and to visit that country than the citizens of the Central Union. Far from being a barrier between the West and East, the Union should become a bridge between Russia and Europe.

It is to the interest of Europe to draw Russia as much as possible into the orbit of its life and to exchange goods and ideas on the largest scale. This aim can be achieved without extending the already vast territories of Russia at the cost of the independence of some small nations.

Any attempt to isolate Russia in any sense whatsoever would be very unwise, and the nations of the Middle Zone realize it as well as anybody. They desire the friendship of Russia and are ready to reciprocate any act of genuine goodwill coming from the stronger party.

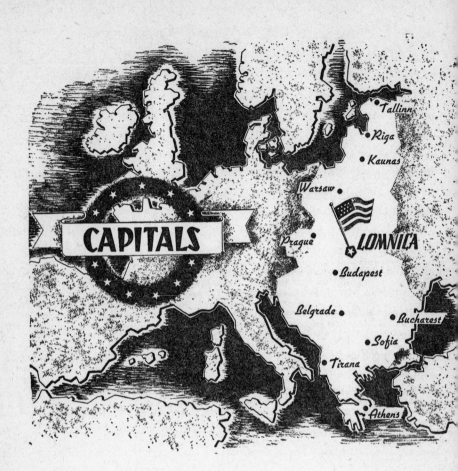

EUROPE'S NEW CAPITAL

THE MIDDLE ZONE should not be governed from a capital outside its geographical boundaries. It needs a nerve-centre of administration and commerce, a federal capital in addition to the national capitals of the member States.

The selection of a capital for the Central Union will not be an easy matter. It is desirable to have a capital centrally situated between the northern and southern parts of the Union. Cracow might be considered, for it is linked by tradition with the whole of Central Europe. It might, however, be a mistake to have the capital in a large country like Poland, as the smaller countries might feel that their claims were being overlooked.

It seems that the best plan would be to create an entirely new capital, a Washington D.C. or a Canberra of Central Europe. The foundation of a new city would provide welcome opportunities for co-operation between the member nations. It might be advisable to establish a federal district which would not belong to any of the member nations in particular, but form their common property.

A good location for such a federal district could be found on the southern slopes of the Carpathians, in the beautiful Tatra Mountains in Slovakia. For instance Lomnica might become the site on which the Union capital might be built by the best architects of Central Europe, working in harmony to erect a symbol of unity and not walls of division.

It is impossible to overestimate the tremendous impression which the establishment of such a capital would make on all the member nations. The nations of the Middle Zone have a keen artistic sense and appreciate æsthetic values. The creation of a new city which would aspire to become the finest in Europe would provide all these nations with a visible symbol of their unity and an object of legitimate pride. If only a fraction of the sums spent every year by the nations of the Middle Zone on arming against each other were devoted to the erection of the federal capital in Lomnica or elsewhere, the new city would soon become one of the best examples of modern planning in the world.

The great wealth of creative talent and skill of the nations of the Middle Zone has never yet been turned to a common task. The results of the teamwork of such a group of highly gifted nations could astonish the world—and themselves.

It is interesting to note that, according to the Office of Production Management of the U.S.A., 53 per cent. of the workers employed in the war industries of America are of Slav descent. It means that they are all natives or descendants of natives of the Middle Zone, for the only Slavs outside the Zone are the Russians, who never emigrated to America, except for a handful of upper-class political *émigrés*. This fact gives a measure of the amount of talent

86

and technical skill which the Central Union could have at its disposal. There is no doubt that the brothers and sisters of the American war workers, who remained in their home countries, have similar ability, which they were unable to develop owing to the troubled political conditions in Europe.

The appreciation of beauty is strong in the hearts of Central Europeans and the vision of a common capital of surpassing splendor could arouse in their minds an enthusiasm of which some more sophisticated nations might not be capable. Such an enthusiasm could help them to abandon petty jealousies for the sake of an idea at once greater and nobler.

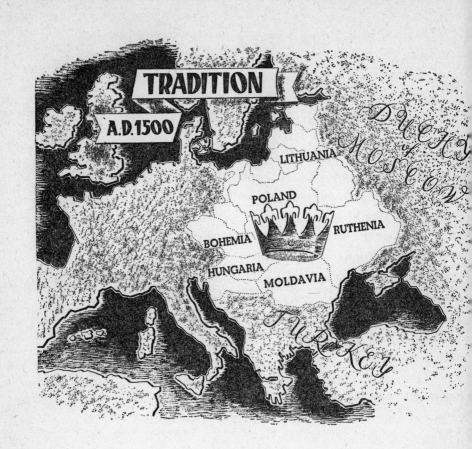

TRADITION

A.D. 1500

LITHUANIA

POLAND

BOHEMIA

RUTHENIA

HUNGARIA

MOLDAVIA

DUCHY of MOSCOW

TURKEY

THE LESSON OF HISTORY

GENERALLY SPEAKING, "historical grounds" for doing this, that or the other, are to be looked upon with some suspicion, for if the future were to be merely a repetition of the past, we should never get very far. Precedent alone can seldom justify anything.

History, nevertheless, governs the present and to some extent the future as well, so it cannot be ignored altogether. In the case of the Middle Zone, the past is to be remembered inasmuch as it has prepared the ground for unity, and forgotten as far as the tradition of strife and discord is concerned.

There were periods of history when large sections of the Middle Zone were united under common rule. The most recent and one of the most significant attempts at integration was that of the Habsburg Empire, which embraced a major part of the Zone. It was, however, a unity imposed from outside, by a German dynasty. Its original shortcoming, ultimately responsible for its downfall, was the fact that the Habsburgs are, after all, Germans, and therefore aliens in the Middle Zone, which is the part of Europe *between* Germany and Russia, but not within either country.

The Habsburg Empire was bound to become, as it did, a tool in the hands of German imperialism, even though its principles of government were different from those of Prussia. The tradition of unity which still exists in the countries ruled by the Habsburgs until 1918 will, however, be an asset in building the Central Union. These countries include Czecho-Slovakia, Hungary and part of Poland, Yugoslavia and Rumania, a large and important section of the Middle Zone.

The fullest integration of the Middle Zone was that achieved in the XVIth century by the Jagiello dynasty of Lithuania. It was all the more remarkable for being achieved, not by wars of conquest, but by marriages and dynastic arrangements, which were the equivalent of international treaties in that era. The Jagiellos ascended the throne of Poland through the marriage of Wladyslaw Jagiello, Grand Duke of Lithuania, with queen Jadwiga, the daughter of Louis d'Anjou, king of Hungary. The result was the union of Poland with Lithuania and, eventually, with Hungary and Bohemia, through the person of the sovereign. The wars with the Turks, as well as the intrigues of the German princes, did not allow the consolidation to become permanent. It is notable, however, that already in the XVIth century the need for the unification of the Middle Zone was realised by some far-sighted statesmen.

The tradition of the unity achieved in the XVIth century under the House of Jagiello can hardly have any

90

practical influence on the politics of to-day, but it provides an interesting historical background for the plan of the Central Union.

Other, more recent examples of international organizations within the Middle Zone could scarcely serve as models. The Little Entente was basically wrong, because it was aimed against a country within the Middle Zone—Hungary—and thus violated the principle of Middle Zone solidarity, which is the condition of survival of all the nations in that part of Europe.

All the pacts and alliances concluded between two or more Middle Zone countries against others should also be forgotten rather than remembered. To unite one half of the Middle Zone to fight the other is merely to hasten the destruction of all nations involved in such a scheme.

THE DUAL MONARCHY

It has been said of the Austro-Hungarian Monarchy that, had it not existed, it would have had to be invented. That statement was approximately true, as it implied the need for integration in Central Europe. There is, however, nothing to suggest that the consolidation of Central Europe can be achieved only under the rule of a dynasty of German origin, such as the Habsburgs. Their restoration is out of the question, but the fact that an important section of the Middle Zone has been united in one State within living memory will be of great assistance in organizing the new Union, although it will be based on very different principles from the old Monarchy.

The Dual Monarchy comprised the entire territories of Czecho-Slovakia, Hungary and Austria, as well as provinces belonging to Yugoslavia, Poland and Rumania. It was a large State (239,980 square miles in 1910) with population of 52,000,000—that is about a half of the population of the Middle Zone at the time. The notable feature of the Austro-Hungarian Monarchy was that the two ruling peoples, Austrians and Magyars, were a minority in the Empire. It is true that the Habsburg rule, almost as harsh as

93

the Prussian in the beginning of the XIXth century, was gradually relaxed during the long reign of Francis Joseph (1848–1916) and eventually became relatively benevolent and mild. Most of the different nationalities included in the Dual Monarchy enjoyed a degree of autonomy and they could use their own language. Nations other than Austria and Hungary—Czechs, Poles, Croats, etc.—were represented in Parliament and their members were occasionally included in the Cabinet. Nevertheless, the two dominant races, German and Magyar, enjoyed a position of privilege, while the Slav nations were relegated to a secondary position.

This system was in complete contradiction to the principle of the Central Union, which would be complete equality of all the member nations and fully democratic governments by majority rule, not by minority.

From the economic point of view, the Austro-Hungarian Monarchy was a successful organisation and it gave a fair degree of prosperity to the territories under its control. Its achievements in that respect can be repeated and improved upon, especially as the possibilities of the Union, embracing several countries which never belonged to the Dual Monarchy, will be much wider.

The tradition of the Habsburg Empire, deserving respect in the economic sphere and to some extent in internal administration, should be completely abandoned as far as foreign policy is concerned. Austro-Hungary played "brilliant second" to Germany—and this was unavoidable, since the Habsburgs are, after all, a German dynasty and the Austrians are a German people. The Central Union must be non-German in its composition. It should include all the lands of the Dual Monarchy, with the exception of Austria itself. Vienna is an attractive city and it has always fascinated the people of Central Europe. It cannot be allowed to become the capital of the Union, for it would then be a centre of German influence. The question whether the Austrians are as bad as the Prussians is irrelevant to this problem. Even if they are honest and peaceful people, their presence within the Union might constitute a real danger, for they might be used by a future Germany as a tool for disrupting and breaking down the Union.

DEMOCRATIC LEADERSHI

THE CONDITION OF SUCCESS

IT IS OBVIOUS even to the simplest minded observer of world events that there can be no peace without the full and unconditional solidarity of the United Nations. Unless we are willing to admit that freedom is doomed to disappear from the world, we must assume that there is only one United Nations foreign policy.

The obstacles to the establishment of the Central Union are many: both external and internal. It would be unreasonable to expect that they could all be overcome by the nations concerned, without outside assistance. Someone should give a lead; but it must be powers that have no selfish, imperialistic interests in Central Europe.

Does it mean that such powers would be acting merely in a philanthropic spirit? Not necessarily. No nation interested in maintaining peace in Europe and the world can afford to remain indifferent to what happens in the Middle Zone, but only some powers may have definite plans of self-aggrandisement in that region. Non-continental powers cannot have any designs of their own on the Middle Zone, while they have very strong reasons to preserve peace in that key section of Europe. Boldness and breadth of vision are indispensable, for mere timid suggestions will never be enough to overcome the inertia of centuries, the tradition of discord and the hostile intrigues of some powers.

The Central Union must be democratic in the true meaning of the word. It can achieve that aim only in the closest collaboration with those countries which provide working models of democracy, perhaps imperfect in detail, but the best that can be found in modern times. Unless Central Europe is to increase the area of the world under totalitarian rule, support and guidance must be sought from the existing democracies.

The suggestion may not appeal to those people in both Britain and America who would gladly be rid of all continental commitments, particularly east of the Rhine. Unfortunately, there is no choice; it is either leadership with all that it involves, or this war will have been fought in vain. There is no other alternative. Inactivity or indifference are bound to result in disaster, for Britain and subsequently America, as well as for Central Europe itself.

Only the joint moral prestige of the United Nations can bring about a genuine reconciliation among the nations of the Middle Zone and induce them to accept mutual settlements, without which solidarity and unity would not be possible. Their moral authority, if they remain faithful to the principles of democracy and the Atlantic Charter, will be a tremendous power.

Split into eleven different States, each surrounded by a tariff barrier, the Middle Zone has hitherto been a negligible market for other countries. Owing to political insecurity, long term investment was inadvisable and the low standard of living of the population limited imports to bare necessities. Unified and developed, the Middle Zone can become commercially one of the more important countries in the world, especially if it abstains from autarchy. The industries of the Middle Zone will have to be developed on a large scale. It would be an error to think that the development of industries would reduce imports from other manufacturing countries. Trade returns show that the major part of international trade is not between industrial countries on the one hand and agricultural ones on the other, but in mutual exchange between industrial countries, because of their far greater purchasing power.

American-British leadership—political and economic—is the vital condition of peace and prosperity for Central Europe.

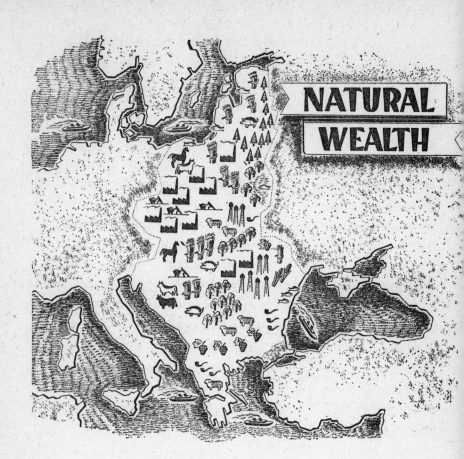

ECONOMIC STRENGTH

THE MIDDLE ZONE is perhaps not a particularly rich part of the earth, but it possesses all that is necessary to give reasonable prosperity to its inhabitants. Most of its countries are agricultural, and that fact forms an additional link between them. They are the peasant countries of Europe and the standard of living of the Central European farmers is more or less the same throughout the Middle Zone. That similarity of social structure and custom will be an asset to the Central Union.

There is coal and iron in Poland and Czecho-Slovakia: there will be more after the return of German Silesia to the Slavs. It seems likely, however, that the Union would not be self-sufficient in production goods and machines, at any rate not for a long time, but such goods could be supplied by America and Britain.

Rumania and Poland have oil. Their supply may not be sufficient for the whole Middle Zone when once it has developed motor traffic up to Western standards. The use of synthetic fuel and alcohol could easily make up the shortage. The Central Union would have enough liquid fuel—the lifeblood of modern transport.

Poland has plenty of zinc and some lead, while Yugoslavia has copper and bauxite (aluminum ore). Rock salt and potassium salts are found in quantity in several parts of the Middle Zone, while the artificial fertiliser industry, using electric power for the production of nitrates, is well-developed in Poland and Czecho-Slovakia.

The supply of timber is adequate and the Union will not have to buy it from abroad. Home grown flax and hemp supplement imported cotton and jute, while the production of wool could easily be increased. Natural silk is produced in several countries and there is an important rayon industry in Poland and Czecho-Slovakia.

The mountain streams, especially those of the Carpathians, can supply cheap electric power. Some of it had been used before 1939, but the possibilities of development are immense.

As to food, the Central Union will have a large surplus left over for export, after feeding its 120,000,000 people. There are possibilities of using alcohol made of potatoes for various synthetic products, such as rubber and plastics. Thanks to the considerable spread of the Middle Zone from north to south, its agricultural products are varied and mutually complementary, ranging from sugar beet, flax, rye, oats and potatoes in the north to grapes, maize, tobacco and fruit in the south. Wheat is grown practically throughout the Middle Zone and stock-breeding has attained a high standard in many countries.

Perhaps the greatest natural wealth of the Middle Zone is its almost inexhaustible supply of skilled and intelligent labor. It used to be described as "cheap," but in the future the level of wages and the standard of living will have to be raised. The Czecho-Slovak industry of pottery and glass, artistic objects and beautifully finished articles of everyday use provides an example of what can be achieved by craftsmen devoted to their work.

Even divided and weighed down by the burden of armaments, the Central European countries have achieved remarkable economic progress in the period between the two wars: 1918–1939. The rate of increase of national income was one of the highest in the world and the economic consequences of the foreign occupation during the XIXth century were being made good with amazing speed. It is obvious that the nations of the Middle Zone will achieve infinitely more when the internal trade barriers have been removed and when security enables them to devote all their energies and talents to the constructive work of peace.

MORAL STRENGTH

MORE IMPORTANT by far than economic strength is moral force. One without the other is powerless, but combined they can achieve much. Moral force is more important than economic resources because factories can be built, money can be borrowed, raw materials can find substitutes, but it is extremely difficult, not to say impossible, to inspire with fortitude and the will to independence a community lacking those qualities.

The Middle Zone, as we have seen, has ample natural resources, and is economically strong. If, however, it lacked moral strength, its natural wealth would be worthless and serve only as loot for anyone willing to pick it up.

War is the test of the moral stamina of nations. Not all the nations of Europe have passed the test with flying colors; if they had, it would mean that the test is easy, which it certainly is not.

Almost every country produced examples of sublime spirit and true greatness. But what we are concerned with is the morale of whole nations, not of individuals or groups.

Poland proved her moral strength by taking up the German challenge, instead of bowing to Hitler's demands, although she knew perfectly well the consequences entailed by such a decision. Poland declined Hitler's offer to march with him against Russia and she remained loyal to her allies at a tremendous cost of blood and sacrifice, without producing a single quisling.

The British nation showed the same qualities of moral strength at the time of the Battle of Britain in 1940, when the idea of capitulation did not even occur to any Briton, although the superiority of the enemy in numbers and equipment was obvious.

Yugoslavia and Greece, hopelessly outnumbered by the invaders, fought valiantly and did not surrender. The epic campaign of the Greeks against the Italians will never be forgotten and the fact that Greece is the smallest of the countries mentioned gives a special meaning to her achievement. As to Yugoslavia, she was handicapped at first by a disloyal government, but by overthrowing it she proved that the instinct of her people was right. The subsequent defence of the country and the campaign of General Mihailovic confirmed the world's high opinion of the Yugoslav spirit. Russia also displayed great courage, and the traditional bravery and fortitude of the Russian people compelled again the admiration of the world.

It is notable that of the European nations which displayed moral strength, three are situated in the Middle Zone. It means that the Middle Zone is not merely a territory with so much coal and so much iron, but also the home of spirited nations, loving their freedom and prepared to defend it at any price.

Such countries cannot be treated as a "sphere of influence" for other powers. Any decision relegating them to the position of protectorates or puppet States would not only be contrary to the elementary principles of justice, but also dangerous from the point of view of international security.

A TIME FOR GREATNESS

SUCH is, in a very brief outline, the position of the Middle Zone in Europe. The establishment of the Central Union will not be an easy task. The obstacles are numerous and some of them appear at the time of writing to be almost unsurmountable, but this should not be a deterrent.

The lack of a common language will be only one of the minor difficulties. One of the Slav languages might be adopted as an auxiliary, as it would be readily intelligible to the majority of the inhabitants of the Middle Zone. The fact that the language spoken on the shores of the Baltic can be understood by people of the Adriatic coast is most significant. If no other grounds existed for the creation of a Central Union, that fact alone should strongly advocate an organisation based on a community of culture and tradition of most of the nations of the Middle Zone.

There was only one great plan of unity conceived by natives of the Middle Zone, not outsiders, aiming at the protection of the entire region against foreign aggression, not at some internal intrigue. It was the plan of the House of Jagiello. The Jagiellos were not the agents of any foreign imperialism—like the Habsburgs—and they extended their domains by peaceful penetration and wise statesmanship, without military conquest. Times have changed and the methods of the XXth century are not those of the Middle Ages, but there are some aspects of the Jagiellonian policy which deserve attention even to-day, such as tolerance and non-intervention in the domestic affairs of other nations.

The nations of the Middle Zone have gone a long way since the days of the Jagiellos and national feeling has become stronger everywhere. Central Europe has shared in the general rise of nationalism in modern times.

It might appear at first that those highly patriotic countries would be troublesome members of an international organisation. The contrary is the case, for precisely the spirit of selfless sacrifice and devotion to an ideal is what is needed to build anything great. A nation willing to fight to the death for its own freedom will also be ready to defend the wider community of the Union; while a nation prepared to strike a bargain over its own independence might well turn traitor to its allies. That is why it is fortunate indeed that there are in the Middle Zone nations which have proved their moral strength and which will inspire all the others with the same ideal of dignity and freedom. They will help to create a new, wider patriotism, not confined by purely national boundaries, and a new citizenship of free men. Tradition may also play its part, but the Central Union will be inspired far more by a bold vision of the future than by any imitation of the past, however glorious.

Victory in the present war will offer to Europe the last chance of settling the vital problem of the continent and averting an irrevocable disaster.

ATLANTIC CHARTER

FIRST, their countries seek no aggrandisement, territorial or other.

SECOND, they desire to see no territorial changes that do not accord with the freely expressed wishes of the peoples concerned.

THIRD, they respect the right of all peoples to choose the form of government under which they will live; and they wish to see sovereign rights and self-government restored to those who have been forcibly deprived of them.

Franklin D Roosevelt—Winston Churchill
1941